Cross Section

1940 entrance

Paleolithic
entrance

modern entrance

HALL OF
THE BULLS

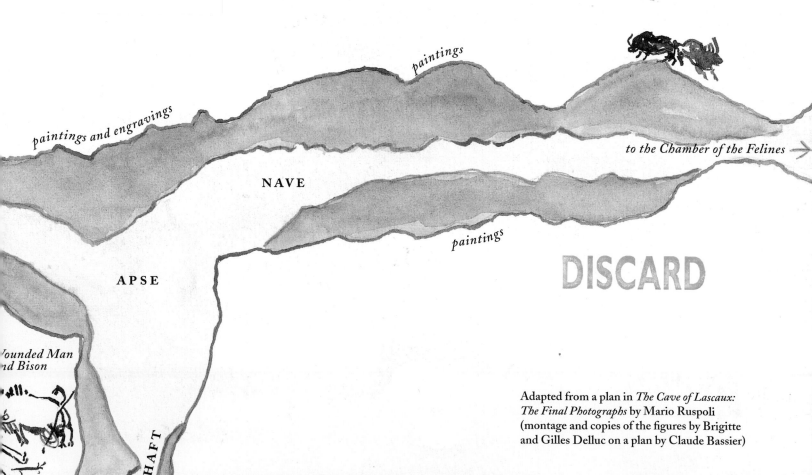

paintings

paintings and engravings

NAVE

to the Chamber of the Felines →

paintings

APSE

DISCARD

Wounded Man
and Bison

SHAFT

Adapted from a plan in *The Cave of Lascaux:
The Final Photographs* by Mario Ruspoli
(montage and copies of the figures by Brigitte
and Gilles Delluc on a plan by Claude Bassier)

THE SECRET CAVE

DISCOVERING LASCAUX

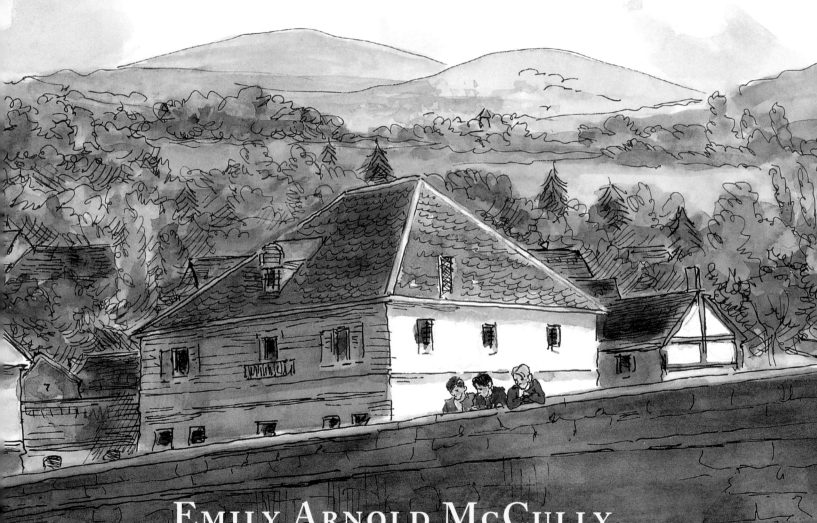

EMILY ARNOLD McCULLY

FARRAR STRAUS GIROUX
NEW YORK

For Liz

Copyright © 2010 by Emily Arnold McCully

Distributed in Canada by D&M Publishers, Inc.
Color separations by Chroma Graphics PTE Ltd.
Printed in May 2010 in China by Macmillan Production (Asia) Ltd.,
Kwun Tong, Kowloon, Hong Kong (supplier code 10)
Designed by Natalie Zanecchia
First edition, 2010
1 3 5 7 9 10 8 6 4 2

www.fsgkidsbooks.com

Library of Congress Cataloging-in-Publication Data
McCully, Emily Arnold.
    The secret cave : discovering Lascaux / Emily Arnold McCully.
        p.   cm.
    ISBN: 978-0-374-36694-0
    1. Lascaux Cave (France)—Juvenile literature.   2. Magdalenian culture—France—Montignac (Dordogne)—
Juvenile literature.   3. Art, Prehistoric—France—Montignac—Juvenile literature.   4. Cave paintings—France—
Montignac—Juvenile literature.   5. Montignac (Dordogne, France)—Antiquities—Juvenile literature.   I. Title.

GN772.3.M3M33 2010
944'.72—dc22
                                                                                    2009014143

PÉRIGORD NOIR

Brive

Montignac

R. Vézère   Les Eyzies   Sarlat

R. Dordogne

Jacques Marsal's teacher, Monsieur Léon Laval, collected prehistoric bones and stone tools from the countryside around where they lived in Montignac, France. Jacques was fascinated by them. He liked to imagine the first true humans, who had lived when woolly mammoths, bison, and reindeer roamed the craggy hills he knew so well.

One day, Monsieur Laval took the class to Font de Gaume, a prehistoric cave discovered decades before, in 1901. As they inched along a narrow passage, the children saw drawings of animals. They seemed to float along the walls, into the inky darkness.

"We are in the presence of the very beginning of art," whispered Monsieur Laval. "For our first ancestors, this was a sacred place."

Jacques noticed initials and a name scratched in French. "Who did this?"

"Years ago, people didn't understand what this was and added their own marks," Monsieur Laval said. "They desecrated this place."

By 1940, when Jacques was a few years older, World War II had begun. The German army had marched across France and captured Paris. The French government had surrendered, but Montignac, in the free zone in southern France, was not yet occupied by the Nazis.

Jacques's best friends were Georges Agnel, nicknamed Jojo, who came from Paris to visit his grandmother in Montignac every year, and Simon Coencas, a Jewish boy also from Paris. They fought mock wars against refugee boys from Lorraine who were housed on a farm outside town.

On September 12, a school holiday, the three were hiding in the hills, keeping an eye out for an "enemy" ambush. They spotted an older boy, Marcel Ravidat, coming up the path.

"Marcel would be a good man for our side," said Jacques. "Hey, Marcel. We're fighting the Lorraines. Want to come along?"

Marcel laughed. "Kid stuff," he said, waving a couple of homemade lamps. He came closer and lowered his voice. "The other day my dog Robot was digging around an uprooted tree. Suddenly, he was gone." Marcel's eyes glinted. "And you won't believe where he went . . ."

"Where?" asked the boys.

"He had fallen into a deep hole. Very deep. I had a hard time getting him out, but I think he found the entrance to the count's tunnel!"

"What's that?" asked Jojo.

"There's an old story that one of the nobles here dug a tunnel from his château and stashed gold in it," Jacques explained. "Forget the Lorraines. Let's help Marcel find the treasure!"

Marcel led them to the fallen tree. They pulled saplings away and hacked at the hole with Marcel's knife until it was big enough for him to squeeze through. He disappeared with a clattering of stones. From far below he called, "Come on."

The others skidded down the shaft and landed on a pile of rubble. There wasn't room to stand.

"This is spooky," muttered Jojo.

Marcel lit one of his lamps and handed it to Jacques. Then he lit one for himself and began crawling along in the dark.

"It keeps going down," he called. They smelled damp clay. Water dripped ominously. Except for the halo of Marcel's homemade lamps, all was blackness.

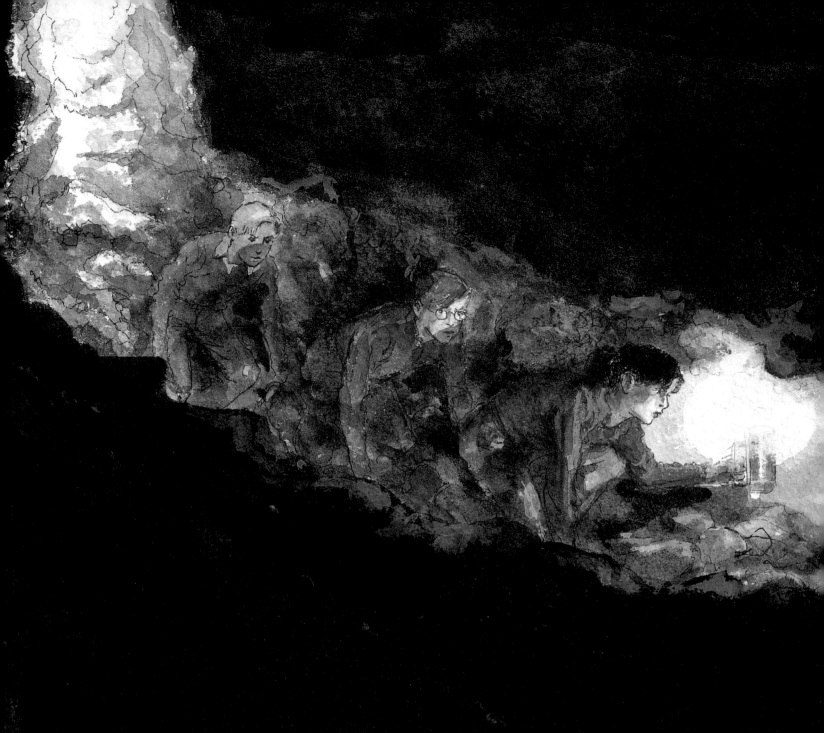

"What if it caves in?" said Simon. "Maybe we shouldn't go any farther."

"You want to wait for us?" Jacques asked him.

"No, but . . ."

"It's as cold as a tomb," said Jojo.

"And wet!" said Jacques.

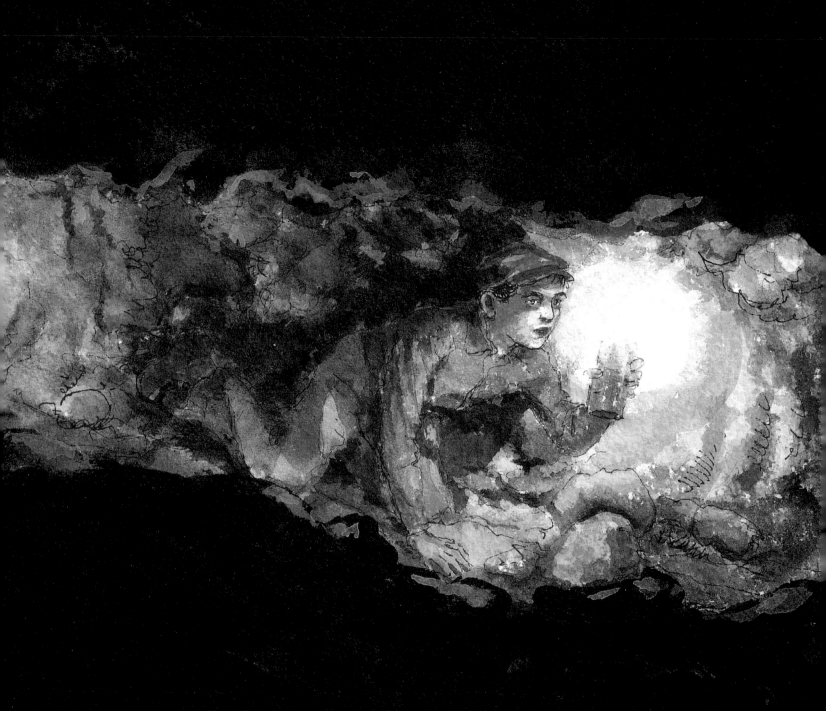

"How will we find our way back?" Simon asked.

"It's a tunnel," said Jacques. "There's only one way to go."

Behind him, Simon whispered, "Jacques—no one even knows we're in here!"

"We can't stop now," Jacques said. He was scared, too. But he was even more excited.

They entered a larger chamber. Marcel's lamp shone on a narrow opening at the end of it. He squeezed through. A moment later, he called out. The others crept forward. They were in a huge cave.

"What's that?" Marcel pointed to red paint on the wall next to the cave's entrance.

Jacques whispered, "It's a cow!" For a moment, the huge beast was terrifying. But it also seemed to watch over them. She will serve as a marker to help us find our way back, Jacques thought.

"What *is* this place?" Simon whispered.

After a moment Jacques spoke. "I know. I think prehistoric people made that picture. My teacher, Monsieur Laval, said caves were their holy places."

As they crept through other passages, their lights revealed more and more animals, some massive, some delicate. Then Jacques held up his lamp and they saw a reindeer on another wall.

"These paintings can't be old," said Marcel. "They look brand-new."

"But animals like these don't live here now," Jacques said.

Turning back, they found that the chamber they had first passed through was also covered with paintings.

No one said a word.

After they climbed out, Marcel took charge again. "We have a lot to explore. Each of you, bring a lamp tomorrow. And remember, you can't tell a soul."

They all swore not to tell anyone.

But the next morning, Simon showed up with his younger brother, Maurice.

Marcel was furious. "He'll have to come. But no more blabbing! This is our cave!"

They found another long tunnel leading away from the main cave. There were more paintings of horses, cows, bulls, and many reindeer.

At the end of a short corridor off the tunnel they found a deep shaft. The four younger boys held a rope for Marcel and he shinnied down it.

"There's a picture of a man with a bird head—he's wounded," he called up to the boys. "And a bison, also wounded."

The others wanted to see the strange images too, so Marcel climbed back out and lowered each of them into the hole. When they were done, he had to haul them up thirty feet because the moisture in the cave had made the rope slippery.

"That's it," said Marcel. "The count's treasure isn't here."

"The treasure is all over the walls," Jacques cried. "My teacher said it's thousands of years old. We have to tell Monsieur Laval about this."

"No!" Marcel said. "We found it! We could charge admission and get rich if it's so great. If we tell people, they'll take it away from us!"

They explored the cave for three more days. When they climbed out on
September 16, a crowd of village children was waiting for them.

Marcel said, "Which of you told about this? It was supposed to be our secret!"

"Too many people know about it," Jacques said. "Let's tell Monsieur Laval now.
He'll know what to do."

Marcel gave him a disgusted look. Then he said, "All right. We'll tell your teacher."

But Monsieur Laval laughed at them. "You went looking for gold and found a painted cave?" he said. "You want to play a joke on an old man?"

Jacques was sick with disappointment. How could his teacher doubt them? Then Monsieur Laval relented. "My former student Georges Estreguil could draw. Take him to the cave and have him make some sketches of your discovery."

The student made careful copies of some of the animals in the main cave. Later, the boys waited as Laval studied them. "All right," he said finally. "Let's go see what you have found."

Nearly every child in town followed them into the cave and waited in suspense to see what Monsieur Laval's verdict would be. In the first great hall, the teacher gasped. "Glorious! These are the finest cave paintings I have ever seen! They are perfectly preserved! This treasure comes straight from our ancestors to all people everywhere!"

He told them that France's greatest expert on prehistoric art, the Abbot Henri Breuil, had fled Paris when it was occupied and was staying nearby. The boys enlarged the entrance some more and added a ladder for the Abbot.

When he saw the paintings, Abbot Breuil said, "I give humble thanks that I lived long enough to see this! Brave boys! I entrust this sacred place to you. Protect it from any who might damage it!"

The boys built a barrier in front of the entrance and slept there in tents every night for months. There would be no graffiti in Lascaux!

Their discovery was reported in newspapers all over the world. World War II raged on, but in the first months, dozens and then hundreds of people came to see the perfectly preserved paintings and to feel their mysterious power. After Jojo and Simon went back to Paris, Marcel and Jacques were proud guides to their treasure. People called them heroes.

After the war, they were put in charge of Lascaux and its millions of visitors. The cave had changed their lives forever.

Jacques Marsal *(bottom left)* and Marcel Ravidat *(bottom right)* sit as Abbot Henri Breuil *(top, third from right)* and other archaeologists view the paintings in the Hall of the Bulls at Lascaux (Photo by APF / Getty Images)

Jacques Marsal and Marcel Ravidat recorded their memories of the discovery of Lascaux. Abbot Henri Breuil and Léon Laval did also. All were interviewed in subsequent decades, which led to varying versions of what happened. This book is a fictional recreation based on anecdotal accounts.

Months after it was discovered, the Lascaux cave was closed because of the war. Jacques Marsal was sent by the German army to a work camp in occupied France. Marcel Ravidat joined the French Resistance. Simon Coencas and his family decided to return to Paris, and although Simon was saved by the French Red Cross, his parents died in a concentration camp. The war prevented Georges Agnel from visiting his grandmother again.

The cave was used by the Resistance as a secret storehouse for munitions. In 1948 Lascaux was reopened, helping to celebrate a new beginning for France and the community of nations. Jacques and Marcel guided the first visitors and were appointed official guardians and guides. Although there were other known caves around Montignac with prehistoric wall paintings, Lascaux was the only one in which the colors had not faded. Sealed for about 17,000 years, it had a protective layer of chalk which made it watertight and kept the approximately 600 paintings and 1,500 engravings from deteriorating. But by 1963, microorganisms tracked in on visitors' shoes, as well as heat and humidity from their bodies and breathing, had begun to ravage the paintings. Lascaux was closed to all but a few scholars. Lascaux II, a meticulous replica of the Great Hall of the Bulls and the Painted Gallery of Lascaux, was opened to the public in 1983.

During the nineteenth century, many people thought the earth was only 6,000 years old. Cave paintings were thought to have been made by pranksters. In 1902, after several caves were discovered in southern France and northern Spain, Édouard Cartailhac, a prominent archaeologist, admitted that he had been wrong to deny that the cave paintings were the work of prehistoric people.

But were the cave paintings art? To these early archaeologists, evolution itself seemed to argue against it. If human abilities evolved just as species did, how could such advanced art be the work of the earliest humans? If not art, what were they? Abbot Henri Breuil proposed that hunters represented their prey in order to gain power over it or increase their bounty. Since then, others have proposed that shamans used the caves for trance rituals. Everyone now agrees that cave paintings are remarkable art. The first appearance of art is reckoned at 35,000 years ago.

The animal shapes often followed the contours of the rock walls. The cave painters probably engraved outlines with flints. They mixed paint colors, usually red, ochre, and black, from plants and minerals. Their paintings were stenciled, blown through pipes, or applied with brushes, rags made of skin or fur, manganese crayon sticks, or fingers. They used stone lamps that burned fats to provide light, and probably built scaffolding to access higher walls.

No photograph can possibly convey the spellbinding power of an actual painted cave.

· BIBLIOGRAPHY ·

Cunliffe, Barry, ed. *The Oxford Illustrated Prehistory of Europe*. New York: Oxford University Press, 1994.

Fanlac, Pierre, and Philippe Davaine. *The Wonderful Discovery of Lascaux*. Translated by Valérie Genta. Périgueux, France: Éditions Fanlac, 2006.

Félix, Thierry. *Le secret des bois de Lascaux*. Sarlat, France: Dolmen Editions, 1990.

Leroi-Gourhan, Arlette, and Jacques Allain. *Lascaux Inconnu*, 12th Supplement to *Gallia Préhistoire*. Paris: Éditions du Centre National de la Recherche Scientifique, 1979.

Ruspoli, Mario. *The Cave of Lascaux: The Final Photographs*. New York: Harry N. Abrams, 1987.

Windels, Fernand. *The Lascaux Cave Paintings*. London: Faber & Faber, 1949.

Don's Maps: Lascaux Cave. http://www.donsmaps.com/lascaux.html.

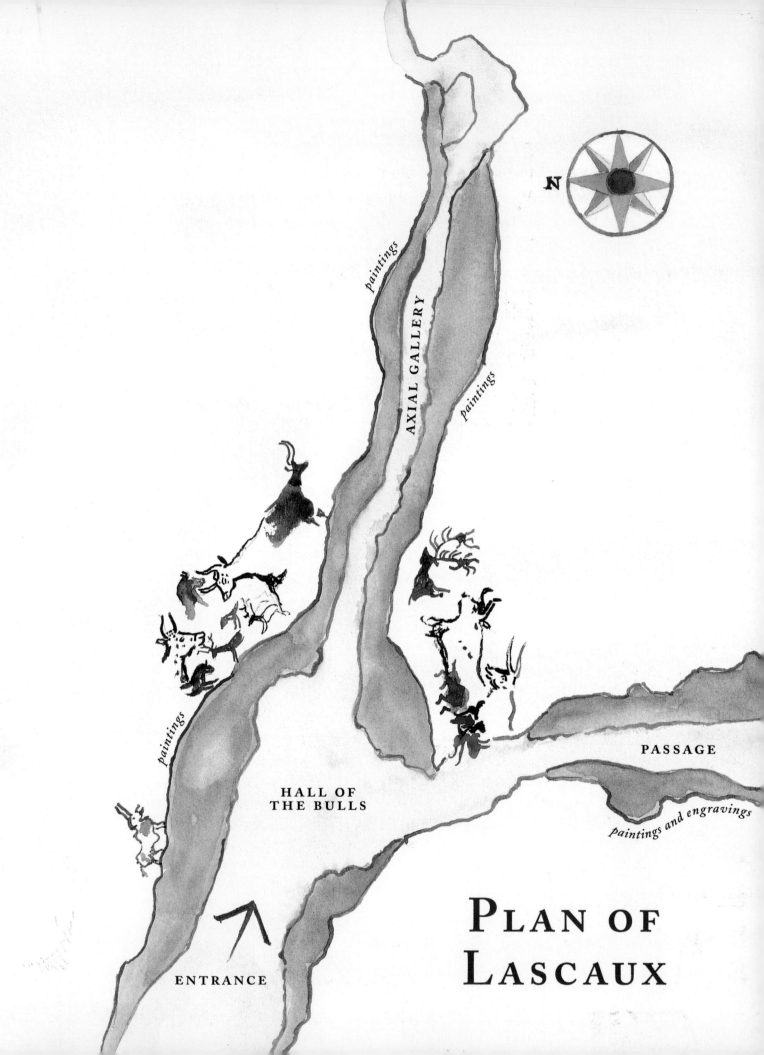

N

AXIAL GALLERY

paintings

paintings

paintings

paintings and engravings

PASSAGE

HALL OF
THE BULLS

PLAN OF
LASCAUX

ENTRANCE